Trivial Pursuit®

SCRATCH & PLAY

2

STERLING

New York / London

www.sterlingpublishing.com

D0205103

STERLING and the distinctive Sterling logo are
registered trademarks of Sterling Publishing Co., Inc.

4   6   8   10   9   7   5

Published by Sterling Publishing Co., Inc.
387 Park Avenue South, New York, NY 10016
© 2007 by Horn Abbot Ltd. and Horn Abbot International Limited. All rights reserved.
Distributed in Canada by Sterling Publishing
℅ Canadian Manda Group, 165 Dufferin Street
Toronto, Ontario, Canada M6K 3H6
Distributed in the United Kingdom by GMC Distribution Services
Castle Place, 166 High Street, Lewes, East Sussex, England BN7 1XU
Distributed in Australia by Capricorn Link (Australia) Pty. Ltd.
P.O. Box 704, Windsor, NSW 2756, Australia

The registered trademark TRIVIAL PURSUIT® and related proprietary rights are
owned by Horn Abbot Ltd. and Horn Abbot International Limited. Used with permission.

Printed in China
All rights reserved

Sterling ISBN-13: 978-1-4027-5089-2
ISBN-10: 1-4027-5089-7

For information about custom editions, special sales, premium and corporate purchases, please
contact Sterling Special Sales Department at 800-805-5489 or specialsales@sterlingpub.com.

CONTENTS

INTRODUCTION

Each TRIVIAL PURSUIT® question in this book (divided into six sections, one for each category on a TRIVIAL PURSUIT card) has four answer choices. Scratch the silver egg next to the answer you believe is correct. If you are right, it will say "+10" and you will earn 10 points. If you are wrong, it will show a negative number from –2 to –5, and you will need to pick again. Keep picking until you choose the correct answer. Once you find the correct answer, subtract the scores for the wrong answers from 10 to get your score for that question. For example, if it takes you three tries, and you get a –3 and a –4 before finding the +10, your score is 10 minus 3 minus 4, for a total of 3. The three wrong answers' numbers always total –10, so if you don't find the correct answer until the fourth try, you score zero for that question.

If you score 1400 or more points total, you're a Trivia Master in a category by yourself!

If you score from 1000 to 1399 points, you're a card-carrying Genus Genius!

If you score from 600 to 999 points, that's not bad, but you might want to take a few more practice laps around a TRIVIAL PURSUIT board!

If you score less than 600 points, console yourself by remembering that the definition of trivia is "unimportant things."

What mountain range is the setting for
The Last of the Mohicans?

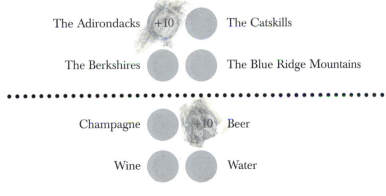

The Adirondacks   +10   The Catskills

The Berkshires   The Blue Ridge Mountains

Champagne   +10   Beer

Wine   Water

What potable do Muscovites refer to as "*peeva*"?

What nation boasts more than 8,000 universities?

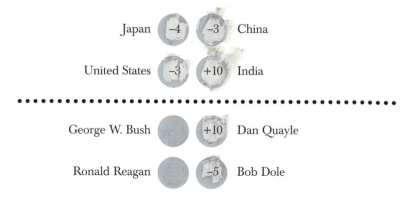

Japan −4 −3 China

United States −3 +10 India

George W. Bush +10 Dan Quayle

Ronald Reagan −5 Bob Dole

Who made a verbal gaffe when he said Republicans "understand the importance of bondage between parent and child"?

What nut do Norwegians hide in their rice pudding as part of New Year's festivities?

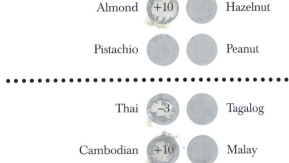

Almond +10   Hazelnut

Pistachio   Peanut

· ·

Thai −3   Tagalog

Cambodian +10   Malay

What Southeast Asian language has more characters than any other alphabet, with 72?

What U.S. state boasts nearly 40 Indian nations within its borders?

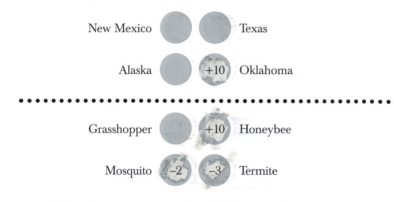

New Mexico ◯ ◯ Texas

Alaska ◯ (+10) Oklahoma

Grasshopper ◯ (+10) Honeybee

Mosquito (–2) (–3) Termite

What European invader did Native Americans
dub "the white man's fly"?

What European nation's flag flies over Tahiti?

France +10   −4 Spain

England   −4 Portugal

· ·

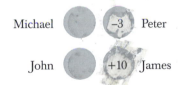

Michael   −3 Peter

John   +10 James

What's Paul McCartney's first name?

What Tuscan stretch of hill towns claims to be the world's first officially defined wine-producing area?

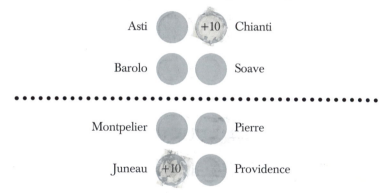

Asti ⬤ (+10) Chianti

Barolo ⬤ ⬤ Soave

Montpelier ⬤ ⬤ Pierre

Juneau (+10) ⬤ Providence

What U.S. state capital has the fewest residents?

What nation enjoys the longest life expectancy, despite
one of the world's highest suicide rates?

Australia   +10   Japan

Canada   −2   Sweden

· ·

Mike Wallace   +10   Andy Rooney

Morley Safer   Harry Reasoner

Who was a regular on *60 Minutes* for 25 years,
or a third of his life, by 1993?

People & Places

What moviemaker did *Playgirl* magazine say had done
more than anyone else to sexualize neuroticism?

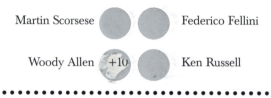

Martin Scorsese ⬤ ⬤ Federico Fellini

Woody Allen +10 ⬤ Ken Russell

· ·

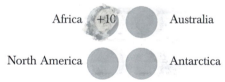

Africa +10 ⬤ Australia

North America ⬤ ⬤ Antarctica

What continent is home to the region
hit by the most lightning?

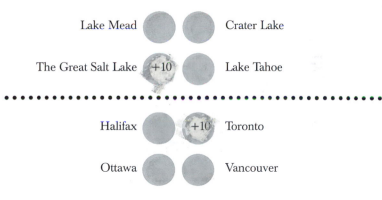

What's the largest U.S. lake west of the Mississippi River?

Lake Mead | | Crater Lake

The Great Salt Lake +10 | | Lake Tahoe

Halifax | +10 Toronto

Ottawa | | Vancouver

What Canadian city did early settlers call York?

What's separated from Australia by the Bass Strait?

The Cook Islands 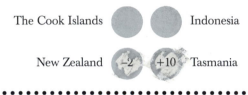 Indonesia

New Zealand −2 +10 Tasmania

· ·

Come ashore  +10 Breathe free

Stand tall Cry out

What are the "huddled masses" inscribed on the
Statue of Liberty's base "yearning" to do?

What Asian nation made the Buriganga River
city of Dhaka its capital in 1971?

Nepal   −3   Cambodia

Bhutan   −3   +10   Bangladesh

• •

Ann Arbor   +10   Kalamazoo

Lansing   −3   −4   Detroit

What Michigan locale is also known as "The Paper City,"
"The Mall City," "The Celery City," and "The Bedding Plant
Capital of the World"?

17

What's the only nation allowed to call its cheese "feta,"
after a 2002 European Commission ruling?

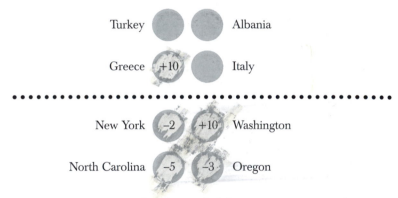

Turkey   Albania

Greece +10   Italy

· ·

New York −2   +10 Washington

North Carolina −5   −3 Oregon

What U.S. state is second only to California in wine production?

What London department store boasts the motto *"Omnia Omnibus Ubique,"* meaning "All Things for All People Everywhere"?

Selfridges   −3   Marks and Spencer

Harrods   +10   −5   John Lewis

Baghdad   +10   Riyadh

Kabul   −3   Beirut

What Arab capital has a name that means "God's gift"?

What midwestern state has its highest point
atop the 4,039-foot Mount Sunflower?

Kansas +10   Indiana

Wisconsin   Nebraska

• •

Norway −3   China

Russia +10   −4   Canada

What nation would you visit to slurp Pepsi
on the icy Kola Peninsula?

What Colorado ghost town shares its name
with the title of a Kevin Costner movie?

Silverado   –3   –4   Postman

Tincup   +10   –3   Fandango

Bicycles   Ukuleles

Automobiles   +10   Cigarettes

What were banned in Boston parks in 1899 after
continually causing horses to run away?

21

What movie first pit the sheepish Tri-Lambs against the lettermen of Alpha Beta?

Porky's (−2) (+10) *Revenge of the Nerds*

Animal House (−5) ( ) *Back to School*

Tom Hanks (+10) ( ) Russell Crowe

Anthony Hopkins ( ) ( ) Jack Nicholson

Who was the first actor since Jimmy Stewart to be nominated five times for a Best Actor Oscar?

What Broadway choreographer created dance moves called the Amoeba, the Drip, and the Zonk?

Twyla Tharp  Tommy Tune

Bob Fosse **+10** Michael Bennett

· ·

Cleopatra *Under Milk Wood*

Who's Afraid of Virginia Woolf? **+10** *The Taming of the Shrew*

What Liz Taylor/Richard Burton movie was the first to boast the classification "Recommended for Mature Audiences"?

What *Melrose Place* star counts Marla Maples as a cousin?

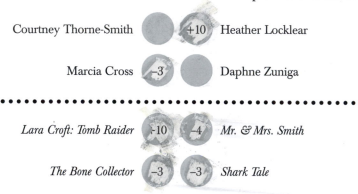

Courtney Thorne-Smith   +10   Heather Locklear

Marcia Cross   –3   Daphne Zuniga

Lara Croft: Tomb Raider   -10   –4   *Mr. & Mrs. Smith*

The Bone Collector   –3   –3   *Shark Tale*

What movie finally gave Angelina Jolie the thrill of
playing opposite her daddy, Jon Voight?

What Jennifer Lopez album was named after
the subway line she rode as a kid?

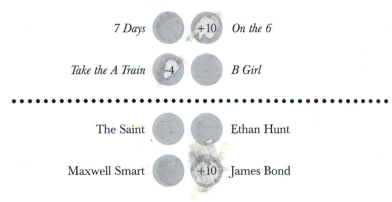

7 Days   +10   *On the 6*

Take the A Train   -4   *B Girl*

The Saint   Ethan Hunt

Maxwell Smart   +10   James Bond

What secret agent's favorite roulette number is the black 17?

What 1975 thriller was the first movie
to open in 1,000 theaters?

The Taking of Pelham One Two Three   *The Stepford Wives*

Jaws +10   *The Omen*

James Cagney   Edward G. Robinson

Burt Lancaster   +10 John Wayne

What legendary Hollywood tough guy converted to
Catholicism on his deathbed, in 1979?

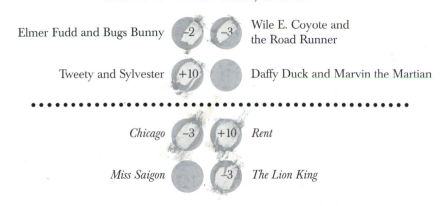

What animated duo debuted in the first Warner Bros. cartoon to win an Oscar, in 1947?

Elmer Fudd and Bugs Bunny −2 −3 Wile E. Coyote and the Road Runner

Tweety and Sylvester +10 Daffy Duck and Marvin the Martian

Chicago −3 +10 Rent

Miss Saigon −3 The Lion King

What Broadway musical set a precedent in the 1990s by selling seats in the first two rows for $20?

What country star, famous for missing gigs, put a vanity tag on his Lexus reading "NO SHOW"?

Merle Haggard   Glen Campbell

George Jones   Hank Williams Jr.

The Glutton Bowl   *Heavyweight Showdown!*

The World Series of Eating   *American Fatty-ators*

What 2002 Fox TV special featured competitors gulping sticks of butter and whole beef tongues?

What freckle-faced 1980s teen star turned down leading roles in *Pretty Woman* and *Ghost*?

Molly Ringwald  Martha Plimpton

Tracey Gold   Jennifer Grey

Huckleberry Hound  Scooby-Doo

Poochie   Ren

What cartoon canine was originally slated to be a bongo-playing pooch named "Too Much"?

What *Three's Company* regular starred in the first American Express "Do You Know Me?" ad?

Joyce DeWitt –3   –4 Suzanne Somers

John Ritter –3   +10 Norman Fell

Law & Order   *Baywatch*

The Simpsons +10   *ER*

What TV series was watched weekly by 60 million people in 60 countries by 2001?

What 1989 Billy Joel hit was included in *Junior Scholastic* magazine as an educational aid?

"Allentown" +10 "We Didn't Start the Fire"

"The Great Wall of China" "Leningrad"

• •

The Rescuers Down Under *Beauty and the Beast*

The Little Mermaid +10 *Oliver & Company*

What 1989 film was the last Disney movie to be animated entirely by hand?

What Mark Twain character recommended curing warts by tossing a dead cat at the devil in a cemetery at midnight?

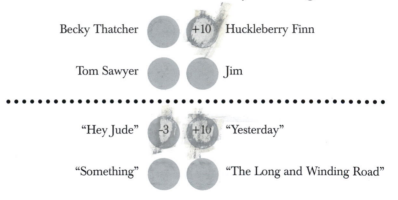

Becky Thatcher ( ) (+10) Huckleberry Finn

Tom Sawyer ( ) ( ) Jim

· ·

"Hey Jude" (-3) (+10) "Yesterday"

"Something" ( ) ( ) "The Long and Winding Road"

What Beatles ballad did *Rolling Stone* pick as the greatest single of the rock era, in 2000?

Who, according to Walt Disney, symbolized "Youth, the Great Unlicked and Uncontaminated"?

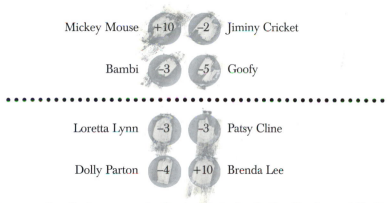

Mickey Mouse +10   −2 Jiminy Cricket

Bambi −3   −5 Goofy

Loretta Lynn −3   −3 Patsy Cline

Dolly Parton −4   +10 Brenda Lee

Who was the first woman inducted into both the Rock and Roll Hall of Fame and the Country Music Hall of Fame?

Who became the first actor to get $30 million for playing the same movie role a third time?

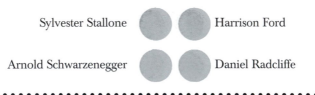

Sylvester Stallone   Harrison Ford

Arnold Schwarzenegger   Daniel Radcliffe

• •

Black & Angry   Bad Attitude

Belly Ache   Bartholomew Aloysius

What did NBC claim the "B.A." stood for in Mr. T's *A-Team* name, "B.A." Baracus?

Which *Sex and the City* character dated Angry Guy,
Speed-Dating Guy, and Marathon Man?

Charlotte   Carrie

Miranda   Samantha

Pottersville   Bedford Falls

Maycomb   Grover's Corners

What town was home to George Bailey,
in *It's a Wonderful Life*?

What 2002 movie sparked lawsuits from Times Square billboard owners when Sony digitally replaced real-life ads with its own?

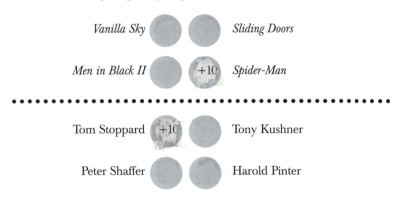

Vanilla Sky   *Sliding Doors*

Men in Black II   +10   *Spider-Man*

Tom Stoppard   +10   Tony Kushner

Peter Shaffer   Harold Pinter

What playwright was given credit for putting words into the Bard's mouth in the 1998 movie *Shakespeare in Love*?

What Greek cartographer first marked positions on a map using longitude and latitude?

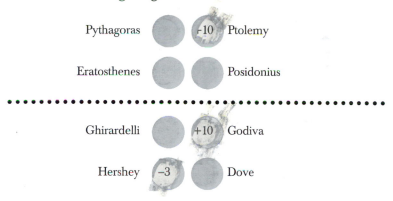

Pythagoras   -10   Ptolemy

Eratosthenes   Posidonius

Ghirardelli   +10   Godiva

Hershey   -3   Dove

What brand of chocolates are made at a plant owned by Campbell Soup in Reading, Pennsylvania?

Who was the first German leader to note: "If the people don't know how laws and sausages are made, they sleep better"?

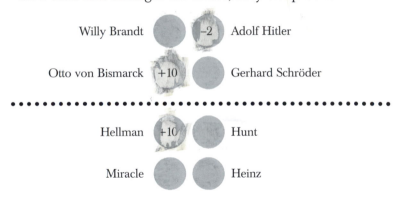

Willy Brandt −2 Adolf Hitler

Otto von Bismarck +10 Gerhard Schröder

Hellman +10 Hunt

Miracle Heinz

What was the last name of the first man to bottle mayonnaise?

What Arab state banned the sale of Pokémon cards in March 2001, claiming they "possessed the minds" of kids?

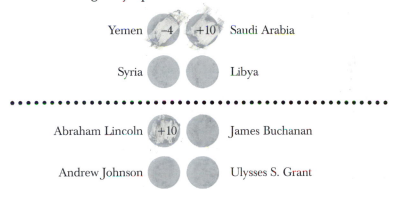

Yemen −4 +10 Saudi Arabia

Syria   Libya

Abraham Lincoln +10   James Buchanan

Andrew Johnson   Ulysses S. Grant

What politician admitted in an April 1859 letter: "I must in candor say that I do not think myself fit for the presidency"?

What U.S. president canceled a planned nationwide conversion to the metric system?

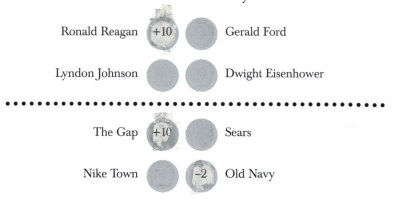

Ronald Reagan +10   Gerald Ford

Lyndon Johnson   Dwight Eisenhower

The Gap +10   Sears

Nike Town   −2   Old Navy

What chain hoped to boost lagging sales by hiring the Coen Brothers to direct a TV ad featuring Christina Ricci and Dennis Hopper?

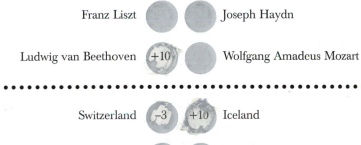

What classical composer died in 1827 of lead poisoning,
according to recent analysis of his hair?

Franz Liszt · Joseph Haydn

Ludwig van Beethoven **+10** · Wolfgang Amadeus Mozart

Switzerland **–3** **+10** Iceland

Ireland · Latvia

What European nation was the world's first
to elect a woman president, in 1980?

Who did William Rehnquist succeed as Chief Justice
of the U.S. Supreme Court, in 1986?

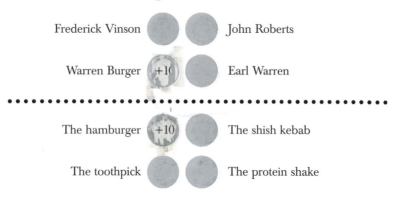

Frederick Vinson   John Roberts

Warren Burger +10   Earl Warren

The hamburger +10   The shish kebab

The toothpick   The protein shake

What did Charles Nagreen claim to have invented in 1885, after his
hard-to-eat meatballs didn't sell at Wisconsin county fairs?

What drink was first bottled in 1894, at Vicksburg, Mississippi's Biedenharn Candy Company?

Moxie   Pepsi-Cola

Coca-Cola +10   Dr Pepper

John F. Street   +10 Rudolph Giuliani

Ron Kirk   Richard M. Daley

What U.S. mayor vetoed a bill legalizing the possession of ferrets, in May 2001?

43

What future U.S. president expelled Eugene O'Neill from Princeton for throwing a beer bottle through his office window?

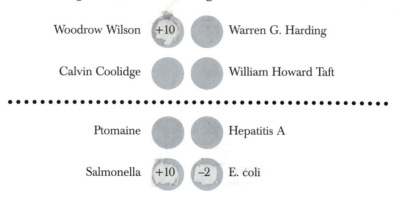

Woodrow Wilson +10   Warren G. Harding

Calvin Coolidge   William Howard Taft

Ptomaine   Hepatitis A

Salmonella +10   −2   E. coli

What microbe, detected in 11 U.S. states, sparked a recall of three million pounds of Malt-O-Meal brand cereals in 1998?

Who led all royalty with 72 fan clubs, by 2001?

Prince Charles   +10   Prince William

Prince Philip   Prince Harry

Montgomery   −4   +10   Tallahassee

Danville   Richmond

What was the only Confederate state capital
never captured by the Union Army?

What newswoman won the battle to land the first 2001 TV interview with Gary Condit?

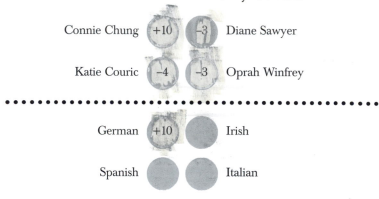

Connie Chung +10 −3 Diane Sawyer

Katie Couric −4 −3 Oprah Winfrey

German +10 Irish

Spanish Italian

What language, in addition to English, did James Garfield give campaign speeches in?

What proposed new name for North Dakota did former Governor Ed Schafer call "a fun idea"?

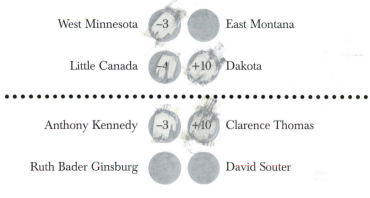

West Minnesota   −3   ⬤   East Montana

Little Canada   −4   +10   Dakota

- -

Anthony Kennedy   −3   +10   Clarence Thomas

Ruth Bader Ginsburg   ⬤   ⬤   David Souter

Who was confirmed to the U.S. Supreme Court by a Senate vote of 52–48, in 1991?

What did the U.S. attorney general declare it okay for women to wear in public, in May 1923?

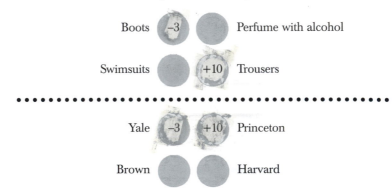

Boots −3

Perfume with alcohol

Swimsuits

+10 Trousers

Yale −3 +10 Princeton

Brown

Harvard

What Ivy League school's trustees voted to ban its annual Nude Olympics, in 1999?

Who was the youngest man to chair the Joint Chiefs of Staff?

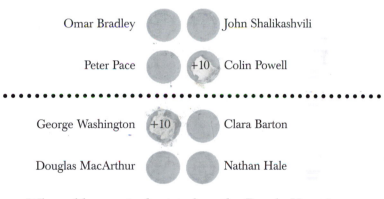

Omar Bradley   John Shalikashvili

Peter Pace   +10 Colin Powell

George Washington +10   Clara Barton

Douglas MacArthur   Nathan Hale

Whose likeness is depicted on the Purple Heart?

What year was Martin Luther King Jr.'s birthday
first observed in all 50 states?

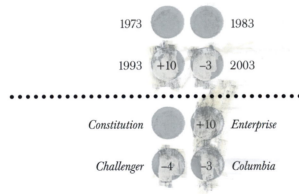

1973

1983

1993 +10

−3 2003

Constitution

+10 *Enterprise*

Challenger −4

−3 *Columbia*

What was the name of the first NASA space shuttle?

What president moved Thanksgiving to
stimulate business in the U.S.?

Franklin Roosevelt +10   Herbert Hoover

Harry S Truman   Dwight Eisenhower

Maine   Kentucky

Virginia   –2   +10   New York

What state has produced the most vice presidents?

What object, 15 billion inches from Earth, recedes
another one-and-a-half inches every year?

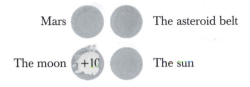

Mars   The asteroid belt

The moon +10   The sun

· ·

Ikebana   Acupuncture

Calligraphy −4   +10 Feng shui

What ancient art utilizes a "*ba-gua*" chart
to locate a structure's nine life areas?

What herb, known to botanists as *Petroselinum crispum*, is often called "nature's mouthwash"?

Spearmint −3   Sorrel

Parsley +10   Anise

. . . .

Sugar −3   Rice

Coffee +10   Corn

What commodity is the second-most traded in the world, after oil?

What do Korean math students count on,
if they're using a system called "chisanbop"?

An abacus 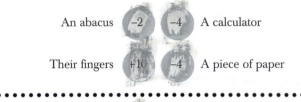 A calculator

Their fingers A piece of paper

Garlic Onion

Leek Shallot

What bulbous edible comes in heirloom varieties like *de vivo*,
Georgia Fire, and Mohawk Valley?

What's the largest bird in North America that builds its nest on the ground?

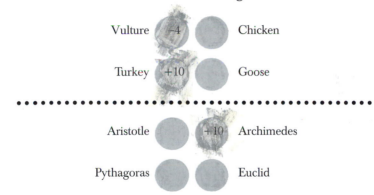

Vulture −4 Chicken

Turkey +10 Goose

Aristotle +10 Archimedes

Pythagoras Euclid

What Greek math whiz titled treatises "On Conoids and Spheroids" and "Quadrature of the Parabola"?

What was the three-letter extension of the
first registered domain name?

gov  edu

com org

· ·

Gerbil  Chincilla

Guinea pig Hamster

What name for the diminutive cavy is
more familiar to rodent fanciers?

What nation do millions of gnus and zebras enter Kenya from each year, in the great Serengeti migration?

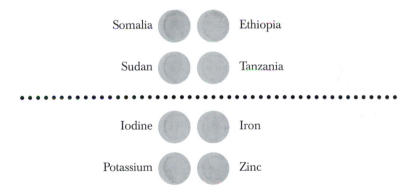

Somalia   Ethiopia

Sudan   Tanzania

Iodine   Iron

Potassium   Zinc

What element does the body need to guard against goiter?

What poison is released when apple seeds are digested?

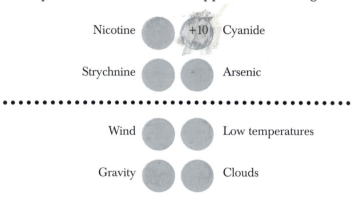

Nicotine   +10   Cyanide

Strychnine   Arsenic

· ·

Wind   Low temperatures

Gravity   Clouds

What scares the chute out of a barophobic sky-diver?

What fruit did the Japanese grow in square containers
and sell for $83 each, in 2001?

Pineapples   –4   Durians

Watermelons   +10   –2   Pumpkins

California   Texas

New York   Florida

What U.S. state gives birders their best chance
to eyeball a mangrove cuckoo?

What root vegetable rich in vitamin C did early sailors
most commonly munch to ward off scurvy,
before the lime was proven effective?

Potato +10   −4 Beet

Carrot −4   −2 Yam

Alligators   Opossums

Florida panthers   Raccoons

What animals most often pester Everglades campers
by chewing through water bottles?

What body part is equipped with the trabecular meshwork, canals of Schlemm, and zonules?

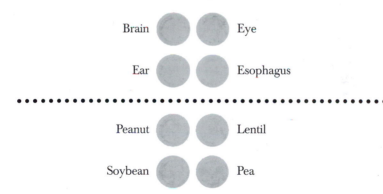

Brain

Eye

Ear

Esophagus

Peanut

Lentil

Soybean

Pea

What versatile legume was the first plant to finish a complete growth cycle, grown from seed until it grew its own seeds, while in space?

What Frank Rose invention from the early 1900s
helps us battle the pesky *Musca domestica*?

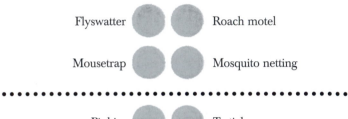

Flyswatter   Roach motel

Mousetrap   Mosquito netting

Pinkies   Testicles

Sets of teeth   Nipples

What does a polyorchid man have at least three of?

What's the largest whale with teeth?

Beluga  Killer whale

Narwhal Sperm whale

· ·

All things English  Chocolate

Alcohol Silence

What does a dipsomaniac crave?

What creatures come in breeds like Australian mist,
Egyptian mau, and Havana brown?

Snakes   Cats

Falcons   Beetles

Aluminum   Tin

Copper   Iron

What's the most abundant metal in Earth's crust?

What company made the first electric dry shaver?

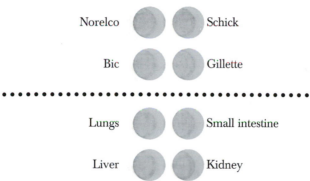

Norelco   Schick

Bic   Gillette

Lungs   Small intestine

Liver   Kidney

What human organ contains thousands of filtering glomeruli?

Who was the first American in space?

Gus Grissom 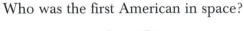 John Glenn

Wally Schirra Alan Shepard

Dishwasher  Refrigerator

Microwave oven Food processor

What kitchen appliance did Albert Einstein secure patents for, but not develop commercially?

Who threw more wild pitches than any
major league pitcher in the 20th century?

Roger Clemens  Mickey Welch

Cy Young Nolan Ryan

• •

Mongolia  India

Turkey Afghanistan

What country's national sport, *buzkashi*, features
players on horses trying to grab a goat carcass?

What fruits give a slivovitz brandy its sweetness?

Plums   Bananas

Peaches   Pears

· ·

Minnesota Vikings   Philadelphia Eagles

Detroit Lions   Carolina Panthers

What NFL team finally won after 12 losses in 2001,
leading Jay Leno to say it was nice to see fans
"hold up their index finger for a change"?

What served as batons in the ancient Olympic
relay race called the *lampadedromia*?

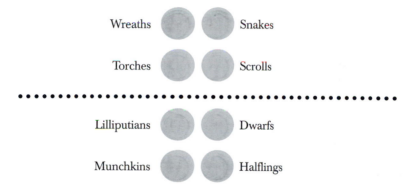

Wreaths   Snakes

Torches   Scrolls

Lilliputians   Dwarfs

Munchkins   Halflings

What did the creators of Dungeons & Dragons rename their hobbits,
after the Tolkien estate threatened to sue?

What Cleveland-born track star was
known as the "Buckeye Bullet"?

Ralph Metcalfe  Mack Robinson

Edwin Moses Jesse Owens

Arm wrestling Darts

Quarters Midget tossing

What sport, organized in 1952 by two friends in a Petaluma bar, got
ABC's Wide World of Sports big ratings in 1969?

What online sword-and-sorcery game was raking in
$46 million a year from 385,000 subscribers, by 2001?

EverQuest   Final Fantasy XI

Asheron's Call   Ultima Online

Bobby Knight   Bear Bryant

Rick Pitino   Joe Paterno

What college coach was the subject of ESPN's
first-ever feature film, *A Season on the Brink*?

What pro wrestler nicknamed his baby daughter "Pebbles"?

Hulk Hogan 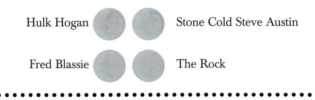 Stone Cold Steve Austin

Fred Blassie The Rock

Asteroids  Tempest

Centipede Missile Command

What vector-graphics successor to Lunar Lander became
Atari's all-time most popular arcade game?

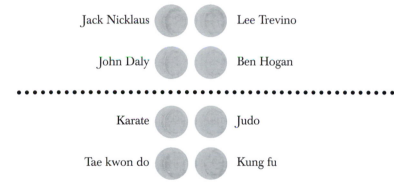

What golfing legend, asked how he knew his way around a course so well, replied: "The holes are numbered"?

Jack Nicklaus   Lee Trevino

John Daly   Ben Hogan

Karate   Judo

Tae kwon do   Kung fu

Which martial art includes the inner thigh technique *Uchi-mata* and the sweeping hip move *Harai-goshi* among its 67 official throws?

What future Hall-of-Fame shortstop played on a Los Angeles high school team with Eddie Murray?

Robin Yount   Ozzie Smith

Dave Concepción   Cal Ripken Jr.

Paris   Madrid

London   Berlin

What European capital filled a stadium with 100,000 square feet of sand in 2002, so folks could play Frisbee and beach volleyball?

Who was the first golfer to win both the U.S. Amateur
and the U.S. Senior Open?

Fuzzy Zoeller  Ben Crenshaw

Arnold Palmer Tom Watson

• •

Detroit Tigers  Boston Red Sox

New York Yankees St. Louis Cardinals

What's the only major-league baseball club with
no player names on its home or road uniforms?

75

What bowl game was featured in the
first national radio broadcast in the U.S.?

Sugar Bowl   Orange Bowl

Cotton Bowl   Rose Bowl

Heisman Trophy   America's Cup

Melbourne Cup   Cy Young Award

What trophy was called the Downtown Athletic Club Award,
when first handed out in 1935?

What Greek town was home to the original Olympics?

Sparta  Rhodes

Athens Olympia

· ·

Lightning  Cyclone

Hurricane Tornado

What meteorological name do the world's
three steepest wooden roller coasters share?

Who was the first American League baseballer to be MVP of the All-Star game a second time?

Cal Ripken Jr. 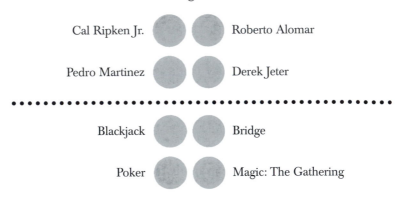 Roberto Alomar

Pedro Martinez Derek Jeter

Blackjack Bridge

Poker Magic: The Gathering

What would-be Olympic sport, according to *The Daily Show*, "combines the fast pace of cards with the athleticism of sitting"?

What type of alcohol provides the punch in a
bottle of the flavored drink Sauzo Diablo?

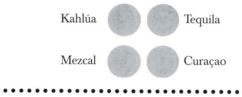

Kahlúa   Tequila

Mezcal   Curaçao

GameCube   Xbox

PlayStation   Dreamcast

What video game console, code-named Dural and Black Belt
during development, was almost called Katana
before a late name change?

What company debuted the Freestyle in 1981, hyping it as the first athletic shoe for women?

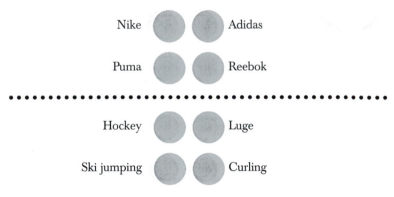

Nike ● ● Adidas

Puma ● ● Reebok

Hockey ● ● Luge

Ski jumping ● ● Curling

What winter sport is contested between the "hog lines"?

Who became the first ballplayer to win Cy Young Awards while on three different teams?

Roger Clemens 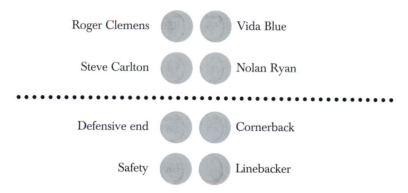 Vida Blue

Steve Carlton   Nolan Ryan

Defensive end   Cornerback

Safety   Linebacker

What football defensive position is dubbed a "rover" or "monster"?

Sports & Leisure

What comic strip appeared in a record 2,000th newspaper in 1984?

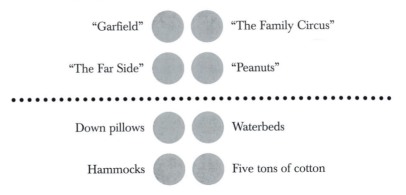

"Garfield"   "The Family Circus"

"The Far Side"   "Peanuts"

Down pillows   Waterbeds

Hammocks   Five tons of cotton

What did Oregon farmer Arie Jongeneel buy for his cows to sleep on, to ease stress on their joints and boost milk production?

What name did Marvel Comics' Norrin Radd adopt to cruise the universe and find planets for Galactus to devour?

Black Bolt 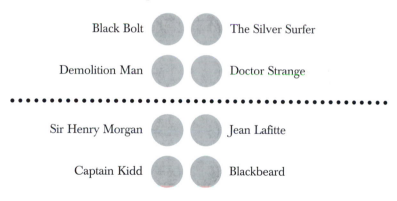 The Silver Surfer

Demolition Man Doctor Strange

Sir Henry Morgan Jean Lafitte

Captain Kidd Blackbeard

What legendary pirate marooned 15 men on Dead Chest Island with only one bottle of rum?

What transparent soft drink resorted to Van Halen's "Right Now" to lure drinkers?

Slice ⬤ ⬤ 7-Up

Tab Clear ⬤ ⬤ Crystal Pepsi

• •

The Itch ⬤ ⬤ The Bedbug

The Squirm ⬤ ⬤ The Funky Chicken Pox

What was the fitting name of a 1954 dance that had folks gyrate while scratching themselves?

Where does a nun place her wimple?

On her head  Around her neck

Around her waist On her feet

· ·

Cocoa Puffs  Kix

Sugar Pops Rice Krispies

What was the first cereal General Mills made with the innovative "puffing gun" they invented in 1937?

What was the favorite cocktail in the U.S. by a landslide, in a 2001 *Bon Appétit* reader survey?

Cosmopolitan 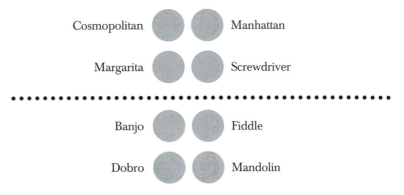 Manhattan

Margarita Screwdriver

Banjo Fiddle

Dobro Mandolin

What traditional bluegrass instrument sports eight strings?

What 1970s fad boasted stickers with names like Blunder Bread, Pepto-Dismal, and Hostage Cupcakes?

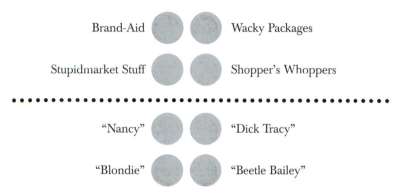

Brand-Aid   Wacky Packages

Stupidmarket Stuff   Shopper's Whoppers

"Nancy"   "Dick Tracy"

"Blondie"   "Beetle Bailey"

What venerable comic strip resorted to a reader contest to name its new character, Chip Gizmo?

What Democrat cringed in horror at his half-brother's role in *Pumpkinhead 2: Blood Wings*?

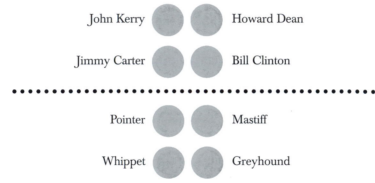

John Kerry ⚬ ⚬ Howard Dean

Jimmy Carter ⚬ ⚬ Bill Clinton

•••

Pointer ⚬ ⚬ Mastiff

Whippet ⚬ ⚬ Greyhound

What short-haired hound is the only breed of dog to earn a mention in the King James Bible?

What "Age of Reason" philosopher kept alert by routinely slamming back 50 cups of coffee a day?

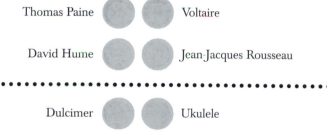

Thomas Paine ○ ○ Voltaire

David Hume ○ ○ Jean-Jacques Rousseau

• •

Dulcimer ○ ○ Ukulele

Viola ○ ○ Lute

What stringed instrument is traditionally tuned to the strains of "My Dog Has Fleas"?

What live-action Disney film did ABC pick for
the world's first digital TV broadcast, in 1998?

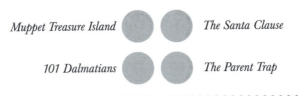

Muppet Treasure Island   *The Santa Clause*

101 Dalmatians   *The Parent Trap*

William Howard Taft   William McKinley

Ben Franklin   Grover Cleveland

Whose ample mug appears on the $1,000 bill?

Who dismissed rumors that she was hurting Derek Jeter's game by dating him, noting: "I'm just a singer, not some magical baseball genie"?

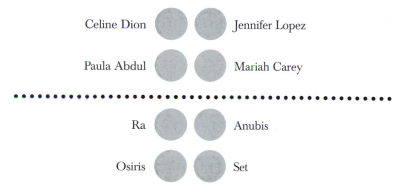

Celine Dion   Jennifer Lopez

Paula Abdul   Mariah Carey

Ra   Anubis

Osiris   Set

What Egyptian god, hacked in pieces and reassembled minus his private parts, nevertheless managed to father a son, Horus?

91

What meataholic rocker titled his cookbook
Kill It and Grill It?

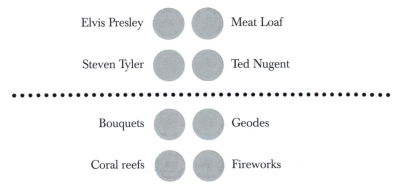

Elvis Presley   Meat Loaf

Steven Tyler   Ted Nugent

Bouquets   Geodes

Coral reefs   Fireworks

What dazzling displays can contain palms, chrysanthemums,
serpentines, and ring shells?

What beautiful young man was a personal
favorite of Aphrodite and Persephone?

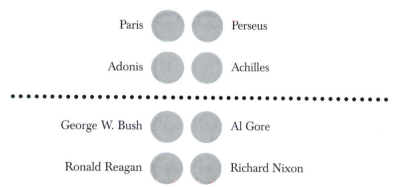

Paris   ◯ ◯   Perseus

Adonis   ◯ ◯   Achilles

• •

George W. Bush   ◯ ◯   Al Gore

Ronald Reagan   ◯ ◯   Richard Nixon

Whose mug was on the best-selling Halloween mask
of a politician, in 2000?

What daily comic strip features occasional visits by
Bob the Dinosaur, "king of the wedgies"?

"Bizarro"   "Get Fuzzy"

"Dilbert"   "Zippy the Pinhead"

• •

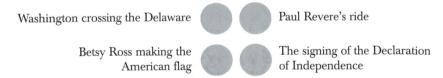

Washington crossing the Delaware   Paul Revere's ride

Betsy Ross making the   The signing of the Declaration
American flag   of Independence

What historical event is shown on the back of a $2 bill?

What basketball star's autobiography is aptly titled *Giant Steps*?

Kareem Abdul-Jabbar 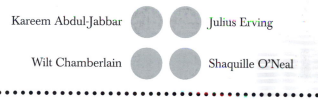 Julius Erving

Wilt Chamberlain Shaquille O'Neal

Dentist  Bedtime

School Chores

What word, the bane of some kids' lives, is derived from the Greek word for leisure?

What's the proper name of the Statue of Liberty?

Lady in the Harbor 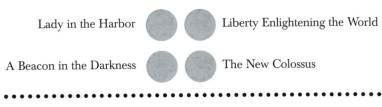 Liberty Enlightening the World

A Beacon in the Darkness The New Colossus

Flowers  Autographs

Cigars Pints of beer

What are candidates for public office in Kansas
not allowed to give away on election day?